Ruth Ellen Kocher's *Archon / After* performs a languid scorching in reverse. Insisting through fragment and association, the question arises: Can there exist a time uncomplicated and unfettered by memory's narrativizing, un-haunted by the inevitable outcome of the meat of the body? There is only complication and turbulence. This rumination is a matter for poetry and physics, for Kocher's incisive language, though the speaker insists, "No language exists safely." There is no safety here. In devastation upon devastation we begin with survival, witnessing the desperation of worry, of "a soul failing to recognize itself walking toward itself," and that "A fragment may never get close enough to itself to be whole again." Do not come to this book expecting any facile answers, come instead to search the mirror of yourself. Expect questions. Expect to "murmur your way back" to your own self.

—Rajiv Mohabir, author of *I Will Not Go: Translations, Transformations, and Chutney Fractals*

Archon / After skillfully "unwraps itself from a meridian of pulpy vertebrae." What I mean to say it's these powerful invocations, their "yearning the perpetuity of return," carry me to what the poem necessitates: a place where Kocher's skilled phrases bring about a guided telepathy that provokes action into a sense-making we desperately need and into which we settle. Kocher's gorgeous and erudite stamina deepen and arrest the poetic line with so much wisdom. Her *Archon / After* is what we require right now.

—Prageeta Sharma, author of *Grief Sequence*

Also by Ruth Ellen Kocher

godhouse (Omnidawn, 2023)

Third Voice (Tupelo Press, 2016)

Ending in Planes (Noemi, 2014)

Goodbye Lyric: The Gigans and Lovely Gun (Sheep Meadow Press, 2014)

domina Un/blued (Tupelo Press, 2013)

One Girl Babylon (New Issues Press, 2003)

When the Moon Knows You're Wandering (New Issues Press, 2002)

Desdemona's Fire (Lotus Press, 1999)

Archon / After

Cover art by Ruth Ellen Kocher

Cover design by Ruth Ellen Kocher and Laura Joakimson
Cover typeface: Courier

Interior design by Laura Joakimson
Interior typeface: Courier and Dapifer

Library of Congress Cataloging-in-Publication Data

Names: Kocher, Ruth Ellen, 1965- author.
Title: Archon / after / by Ruth Ellen Kocher.
Description: Oakland, California : Omnidawn Publishing, 2024. | Summary: "
A surreal poetry collection considering memory and self-discovery
through the character of the archon, the keeper of the mental archive.
In Ruth Ellen Kocher's Archon / After, the archive is revealed as both a
form of violence and of memory, of site and of event. As keeper of the
archive, Kocher's archon determines what pieces of the past may be
preserved, housed, documented, ordered, and reviewed. Through these
poems, the archon dives deep into memories and into the mysteries of
daily life, and, in governance over the future, determines what will be
and should be forgotten. The act of forgetting becomes archival
violence, with the archon not only serving as the guardian of what
remains in the archive but also as an eradicator who decides what is
purged. The imagistic and surreal language of this collection invites us
to explore a non-logical terrain as we follow the protagonist into her
darkest memories and find a path for our own journey of self-discovery.
"-- Provided by publisher.
Identifiers: LCCN 2024028641 | ISBN 9781632431578 (trade paperback)
Subjects: BISAC: POETRY / General | POETRY / American / African Ameri-
can & Black | LCGFT: Poetry.
Classification: LCC PS3561.O313 A88 2024 | DDC 811/.54--dc23/eng/20240624
LC record available at https://lccn.loc.gov/2024028641

Published by Omnidawn Publishing, Oakland, California
www.omnidawn.com
10 9 8 7 6 5 4 3 2 1
ISBN: 978-1-63243-157-8

Archon / After

by

Ruth Ellen Kocher

OMNIDAWN PUBLISHING
OAKLAND, CALIFORNIA
2024

TOC

Forward

Afterword

He doesn't know I hate love,

possess it as an obliterating missile,
sanctuary its casualties, inhabit the violence cluttering its wake.

I'm also destruction.

He kisses me, anyway.

He moves to possess my crest and break, defers the skunk-gut
skidding the side of the road as testament to earth's repertoire of
release, blood light sparking as dark shuts horizon for someone,
somewhere, alone, sipping Matcha, wondering about the last
election and how death has become cliché.

He asks, *will you make me a sandwich*...

I pitch regret, curtain my portal-ed departure, feast on gaze until
I'm sated-sick, *you're so ... pretty,* said as dispossessed denial or
fever dispelling the body.

He never figures out I'm more event than possession, more
whiskey than smoke.

I'm eclipse divining an arrow to the heart.

I never write of him again.

1.1

After

The impossibility of what happened is sum,

solved in retrospect, like the three of swords reversed, which is to say, a heart spliced by three knives pointed away from an upward abyss, a symmetrically lodged triad, piercing red flesh though   spirit   most.

Not a single drop of blood falls either from the heart or the blades, which is to say, in one deck the heart is a claw embracing last life and in another deck the heart is a blue tone speckled in shadow as though it is the body holding its breath as spirit frees itself from that fault, unwraps itself from a meridian of pulpy vertebrae, spindles itself at last and but again to magnetic drift yearning the perpetuity of *return*.

A cosmos might happen in the wilderness a heart makes of blood against the ghostly rigor of stars, a happening inertia less a kind of stillness and more a flock of geese suspended in reverse flight, the paddle   of   their   wings   also   reversing   sky.

What happens is still, a not-happening, a not-yelling through the stairwell of your home in winter's dead hour

—*Get out*—

a long and extended vowel clearly indicated by a crow perched on top of a heart-shaped ribcage, red and divining, a drift equation of before/after.

_____

12.30

I can't make a single word mean *it never happened.*

I can't make a witness.

I can't make a fern or carpet the forest likewise between two paths
that never meet but follow the flank to the ridge.

The ridge overlooks another river.

I can't make a word mean *every man who has never killed me* because
the room would be un-full.

The word could never stay.

The house wouldn't have it either.

I can't make a word mean *all you ever did was build a way out.*

Every word means escape a ruined architecture of dresses squared/
squared against the staircase of our coming and going, always
ascending.

I can't break a word if *she is a fiction unconcerned with the beginning*
because lore is useless.

The evening cleaves.

My shoulders and I have mistaken the blueprint of my heart. An impossible liability.

I can't snip out the bitter or map my core, or intervene on my own behalf.

Eventually I'll style *bitter* an ordinary thing, a salve.

I never mean to hate mock orange

                            in the way Glück makes me feel I should, its
poor white areola helplessly circling butter-yellow tufts.

Shorthand defeat, evident bow.

That year, in the library, I incant the lines she wraps loosely around
my stems: *I hate them / I hate them as I hate sex / the man's mouth/
sealing my mouth, the man's / paralyzing body.*

I don't understand but incant, again, ivory-ego, anti-everything,
retro-poetic-smirk, not-accidentally over-learned little pebble-brain.

Cranial gangster cos-play.

I have not-enough-to-say about post-century-anything.

I want her to be wrong about flowers and sex and men but I don't put
her back, don't retrieve the words or make them alien and bruised.

I molder them in my mouth.

I taste her for the rest of my life.

25

12.2

The latest trend on the app is *stitch this video and*

tell us the absolute worst thing a man has ever said to you which becomes a viral *and then* combination of qualifications *and he thought it was a compliment* . . . or . . . *right after you had sex* . . . or . . . *that he thought was sexy but was really a threat.*

I dismember within a body, magic all cells into a confetti sparkling, teaming under-kin.

Call it an anxious hilltop mounding beneath my diaphragm or call it a pantheon of butterflies dismantling the constellation of utterances I hold, the man's voice always the same, idle or wispy pandemonium: *how old are you* . . . *if you were just a little smaller* . . . *you're so tiny.*

Respiration is never part of this recall but yes, the heart bobble, the way the stomach seems to recede further inside.

Call me when you turn 16 . . . *that mouth* . . .

No language exists safely.

No moon is just a moon.

No distance is far enough.

He says, *lithe* and I am broken for ten more years.

You're beautiful I hear as a threat, as carcinogen, a concern reclined,
inventory:

closest door ...

11.4

When I die alone I want mostly to be

at least partly clad, at least a bra, a black one because black is intentional.

I want to be lying on my side.

No.

I want to be lying on my back with my legs crossed at the ankle, jaw extended up a bit as though I were just lying in the sun thinking about the past, thinking about how only the dead will interrupt this moment, my neck flexed just enough so the shadow of my jaw seems a mercy as my silhouette blooms into an eternal pose.

I want the carpet under me to rhyme with the late October roses blooming blood red in my yard long after their leaves have curled yellow back towards under-stem.

As I die alone, the memory of those roses will be a murmur circling the room: *she was so young* or *she lived so long* or *she was a plume, a spur of pleas drenched in midnight, she was a notion of bones that had been a woman* or *she ate the wind as though it filled her.*

I'd like my toes to be painted any color of pink-opaque that interrupts the way death stitches my body blue.

I want birds as morning-marquee, a sky-circling murmuration.

I want mercy, mostly.

A soft-landing-parachute into forever like soul-strike, like posed-riot, then, home.

10.28

I look up the word *euphemism*,

                                   not ever trusting what I remember it to mean,
or resist its meaning, or imagine as a nigh region of my body's angular
gyrus where a blue tangle of basal ganglia amplifies my cortex against
perpetual loss.

Some storefront with cafe chairs like the ones they use in Bryant Park,
only black.

Chairs circling small tables.

A red hydrant out front, so, no cars.

No city.

Coffee.

Pizza.

The sky is never bright in the corners of this soon-to-be failing
because nature meters magic in barely digestible doses, small episodic
lilies flanking the recall of a road somewhere with someone.

Someone may have loved *someone* who didn't love *her* back, a better
loss then, a thorn that leaves a little scar on my thumb so I see it and
see again tenderness come through the door and hand me roses.

I clutch at them so completely, I bleed a little.

My husbands have all been left foot reckless, said, *you are she.*

I believed them.

I believed *don't tell.*

I bedded down the triggers.

I reformed my sleep and welcomed the gazelle that bounded from my dream but didn't follow her.

One husband was an amber fissure whose identity remains a mystery.

One, a rabbit hole.

One, a bone that breaks the skin.

One, a courthouse waiting to happen.

One, an orange under-light, think lava or sun in a movie about catastrophe.

One, a mangy cowboy lifting me out of the sea of my childhood.

One, an algorithm for *I never want enough.*

She, also, crashed.

She also hated him as they hated each other slightly more than they hated her.

Not my fissure.

Not my grip.

Not my root chakra balancing above their dew-skin as I closed their portals, lacquered calm their rage.

He was a darling in the fist of morning.

He was a sleeve of lies.

He, also, resented my bark, my hope-thing, my mediation of his determined implosion, my barely singed inner edges.

There is a plant on my sill I look at every morning and feel content not knowing its name.

One, so hard to recognize for who he says she was before *I say*, too nicely, sibilant fricative spit on my lip, *leave, soon, peace be upon him, and him, soon, her, and she.*

10.7

Jane is on a road trip

which is entirely blue-velvet-moto-jacket-
boss of her.

Jane's a badass metaphor, always well-deep in the phenomena of what
an utterance can do to a piece of fruit, to a maple infested by bees i.e.,
honey.

An utterance might be *dappled cherries*.

Another might be *how to kill bees humanely* or *it was a pomegranate
mistaken for an apple*.

I try to avoid returning to Eve which seems inevitable if I begin with
Jane—but, mystic shift.

Into-ness.

Ghost-locus-solstice rumble of crevice.

CASINO-daddy-big-dick-energy, like *trophy* but *drift*, like *clamp the
dead in place* or *after the procedure, the infection was more a ribbon
around her spine instead of a sleeve*.

I lean into Jane, dialogue of flame.

She holds a helmet in one hand, a knife in the other.

35

A poet I not-so-secretly love writes, *maybe I am / a suitcase unspoken for*

which I misread, out loud, as   *a suitcase alone*
like I've read the solitude beneath him instead of the words, feel his
body pause between each breath in a room where he writes   *alone*
against the peril from which poets beg poems to save us.

I'm guilty of fluent swoon, the thrown-down heart, the rot romance
makes of kindness in a poem which asks so little, which appears full-
faced on the page, wanting just a little respect.

I don't tell this guy, whose come to me like a river forever forward
cresting against moss, hulking a far edge not knowing when it will
arrive—I don't say *your wound is not yet angry.*

I don't say *there is nothing kind about a poem,* or *the poem cannot love you
back* because he is a violence that hasn't happened.

He is a pistol.

There's a young white man in America, an explosion asleep in the
cradle the poem will make of him.

He's jones-ing for an ebb-thing that will lie, say *this poem is frail, like you.* So, I say.

This morning a poet sent an email signed

—in love and lipstick --it made me so happy to remember there are poets in the world who wear lipstick, who sheer woe and walk barefoot on fractured earth, who weed peril.

I'm sometimes that kind.

I share *lip smackers* with Donna who teaches me at 14 that magenta belongs everywhere

—magenta relocates fear—

Smudged mascara makes a lust of grass.

We think she has beautiful legs.

We think I have beautiful teeth.

We don't know what it is but it happens.

Each night, blush-perfect.

A poet who wears lipstick coagulates summer into a truce between an affable sigh and a wail.

(pinched from sky's blue palette)

Red fatal-femme.

I ask her to write a poem without using the word "I"

It's my weakness—even here, where I
multiply myself by six before ending a single sentence as utterance
makes me epoch, makes history, makes *a person's life* among scant
nights when I relish not knowing myself (in someone's arms) because
personhood remains a privilege.

I don't tell her I know the wilderness of interior, the way she might arch
in sleep with erratic *undoing,* how I'm just now realizing mastery
and mothering are the same kind of theft.

I say *hope* but mean *plenty.*

When I say *generation* she hears *surveillance,* as in *She is prone to a*
surveillance of stars, as in *He squalls the rumor of his birth,* or *Somewhere a*
badger takes a train that crosses a bridge and dreams of "I" as though "I" will
make her someone's life—a vertiginous slack-self un-being.

I dream of Noah sitting in his best posture

                              across from me, hands folded, a cream colored
short-sleeved Oxford button-up, pressed.

Noah's hair all silver, neatly coiffed, looking like a high school science
teacher, expressionless, not flat. Clean-shaven.

Think, *Aqua Shave.*

Think, *pleaser.*

I wake, think *he made it,* by which I mean, he's no longer stuck in the
shudder of death, no longer seized in life's withdrawal nor moved to
cleave ashes his body becomes.

Somewhere, before him, I pass a dark city where every building looks
the same, a shoebox standing on end painted black with colored
streaks as though children were their architects.

There are no windows or grass.

Children seldom remember what they believe imagines itself into
being.

They may think toward an *order of things* like snow is a side effect
of Christmas or lemonade means something other than citrus always
growing somewhere on trees.

I meet him a year after my first divorce when I long for heels, crave
shimmer, feel my quake lay bare foothills and mourning.

Noah never knew.

42

My father's sister dies on his birthday when she is 48,

when I am 16, almost 17, when my father is 42, when
the phone next to my bed is powder blue and shaped like a donut,
when the stove is avocado green and battles for control of the house,
not a house.

We say *house* but mean apartment as though we can reverse-Jericho
walls around us.

Yesterday, my aunt died on my birthday.

I was turning something-something and she was not yet sixty-
something, smaller than she'd ever been, dimmed as death's glamour
filled her body's conviction for fatigue, for heart stop, for the slowed
down loon in her distance to go silent as wood.

When I was 9 and she was some-kind-of-teen, she got drunk on my
grandmother's birthday, called her Sloe Gin *champagne* and yelled in
the face of every man in our family.

*Your boots are ugly your breath stinks I never liked you—I've been waiting
my whole life to tell you I do not like you.*

They heard her.

The white pine heard her, too, sun streaking the trailer window that also leaned in closer to listen.

Each wolf-cut lineage of square-ish men, heard her, took her sot-logic, felt the years divide impervious to either desire or grief or the dips of chokecherry-shadow out back.

Each month my aunt's daughter calls to say she has not yet died until one day she calls to say she has finally died and also:

I don't know what to say but know she loved you.

I'm eating lemon birthday cake alone on my deck watching a fly struggle on the screen.

I don't know how old her daughter is this day, the day her mother dies.

She doesn't know me by years, either.

44

7.27

The app I download for meditation is

a solid orange meditation surrounded by
meditating angles, a circle, orange, a square, orange.

I never open it, just look at the little icon.

A softened deeper orange.

The round suggestion of a particular citizen of an orange republic.

A golden moon not quite golden.

A tense skip of pink sand in shade.

The quietest of hydrangeas bowing east.

The soft not-so-much pink gum of the groundhog out by the shed.

Tiny orange seizure.

Brain blurt.

Little third eye.

Mimosa tree-tufting a hill.

And so on—*orange blurt. orange cat, orange incident.*

The search results for seizure include: *What causes a seizure to happen What are the symptoms of a seizure What are the types of seizure What happens when you have a seizure.*

Not all seizures are orange or egregiously sweet.

Not all end in wastelands or twilight sleep.

46

One might be a tremor of bicycle spokes.

Another, the sound of tracks beneath a train.

I can't find an end for orange or the way it spheres the seizure's silence.

I look up *emeshed,*

                    a misspelling for *enmeshed* though it's
impossible not to understand how entanglement feels regardless of the
spelling.

I recognized him but he didn't recognize me.

Vague, I know.

Tattoos halo his neck, vine his arms, hands, his fingers, not so much
cupping a cigarette but huddled around it.

His Wikipedia is a funeral, a digital yawn of analog life, a slip into
bodacious-embrace, forever-from-this-day-forward, uncomplicated
assemblage, after-being cloaked in personhood.

Clamor *hallelujah—*

He didn't love me.

He didn't think of me while he sobbed in his car last spring.

He apologized to the dashboard for the impetuous way shadow gleans
light.

I look up *gleans*—the correct spelling for *gleens*.

This year, I try harder than any other year not to die.

I look up *forgive.*

I make no sense in remaking him.

When the call comes, I hear myself wail as though I feel great pain.

When I am in the yard,

when my neighbor walks by, when she asks *what kind of lilies,* when I look up to see another skinny white woman.

I say, *Summer Lilies*

Tiger Lilies, she says back.

Have I mistaken *Tiger Lilies* for *Summer Lilies* or can I no longer tell the difference between one skinny white woman and another skinny white woman as though skinny is as much *true nature* as *white* and *tiger*.

I'm not so much wrong about my own flowers as I am not skinny or white.

She is one foot forward looking back, the air between suspended in tilt-a-whirl gravity and a colonial grin.

She is milky, a flash, minnows on a lake.

I am July again when a phantom circles every summer nightmare damp.

Starfish is not a lily—I say out loud—*but should be, like Stargazer's imbecile cousin.*

She's gone, my soliloquy, rising.

Shale is the earth's flare failing beneath her crust, flailing at the feet of an ice age, which she doesn't hear though the lilies swoon.

Dolphins make a pillory of the ocean's surface.

Yesterday was a car door.

Tomorrow is a truck.

The lilies would say *surrender* if they could, would lumber, planetary, in loose orbit around me, constellations of tangerine-touch.

A *Spider Lily would be wiry and black,* I want to say but don't, and also, *a failing-shard-moon black-mask above my house.*

Her house, too. Our houses.

6.8

I worry everyone I've known has been the same person --

a single fragment, a thousand cramped bodies, a
thousand more.

Within this worry, a soul fails to recognize itself walking toward
itself.

A fragment may never get close enough to itself to be whole again.

It's true.

I worry about everything.

I worry I won't again see Pittsburgh's yellow bridges scalloped against
the low gray heaven of northeast-sky.

I left her in the last thick summer night I remember before leaving for
college and, now, here she is, a life later, bagging my groceries as a
teenage boy with horrible beauty, the same eyes under the same brow
as though a temporal meadow of *then & now* means a body might
forget the plurals of being someone somewhere else she'd always been,
somewhere she never knew.

6.6

Michele tells us her mob name is Velvet

I understand what it means to feel jealous.

It's the possibility of an other-object gushing through the sluices of a never-named you.

A *you*, unpinned.

The anonymity in being "named for," as in, *commit to a life on the lam, incognito.*

To be named for your father completes a room like curtains.

To be named for your aunt means a low flying anonymity somewhere in her past, a time she believed she could be un-seen *in the blink of an eye.*

In one story you name your daughter *dutiful.*

You name your daughter, *beloved,* name her *friend.*

In another story, you name your daughter *mother*—naming to undo.

Or, naming a stitch like the binding of what's done.

A once-friend changed her name but I've forgotten why which means I've also forgotten her name.

Your mother's name is a quilt she'll buy, velvet-purple velvet-green, duende flapping black wings.

I would like to be called *Velvet*.

I'd like to mouse the uneven night and manifest elsewhere, name myself some scene.

I'll never be my own story.

Someone, somewhere, is named Hot Pink, her clipped hair the color of beet juice, her walk, a specific movement.

Hot Pink caterwauls the resonant evening at will, all stunt, plumb like a good doorway my mother walks through to meet her own mother again.

One of them holds me close but I can't remember who.

I think about my name too often.

One of them thinks, too much, how to name.

6.15

Each boy adores Kerouac,

first crush, peacock *Beat-party-trivia.*

Then, Dungeons and Dragons.

I parallel my trips through universe looking for a past life or June Jordan.

Her ghost lifts all the trees in a courtyard while poets pray her name.

I expect magic when poets die.

My body, indifferent to other plush bodies.

The great flood won't see me coming.

I roam that destruction.

My soul grows faster than my faith.

You're invisible.

You witness.

You stupidly give away fire, stupidly scorch horizon.

No boy could save Anne Sexton.

They couldn't ascend her sorrow, her sagging, inevitable droop.

They couldn't distinguish *pinnacular* from a small conical lie.

It takes so little to impress me: brown corduroys, Camus in his pocket.

He talks about Ginsberg and the ballet teacher who molests his adolescence.

You really are beautiful.

He rubs the tendon taught from his thigh to groin to show me how she'd begin.

6.8

Is it true that in the 80s

you were more likely to be killed by a serial
killer if you had long hair.

Is it that to be killed by a serial killer means your grave will never
settle but remain a cavern around your expired bones.

It is true that I fall in love with him because he knows the names of
all the flowers and all the birds, whispers them out loud as he falls
into sleep, *delphinium, aster, house finch, mockingbird, scrub jay.*

It is true that a caterpillar follows my scent one July as I sit naked
along the bank of the Allegheny so when I stand and walk a few steps
away it stands on one blunt end clawing the air with a hundred blind
legs trying to grasp my musk.

It is true that when we are all naked, I noticed how I am noticed, how
I become someone's, how a gaze sets against my neck so, even at a
distance, I feel a jaw clench.

It is true I loved her ache and casual grief, that she spoke of being
killed often, as we all did, as though rehearsing our headlines would
augment the future in our favor.

Is it true that as he threatened me, he reached to push his glasses up
the bridge of his nose like a boy.

Yes, it's true.

Everything is more beautiful after, forever, and so.

It's true that we shed our virginities like snake skin in early summer.

We fled from the malodorous reach backward into beginning.

Is it true that twilight blisters my memory so nothing awful ever
happens once it does.

Every June liberates every pond peeping and mossed.

Every stamen fists the night.

Is it true that in the 80s I hung up my childhood as though it were a
slip of sleep and mortar, a rhyme, then done.

It is true that dust remains forever pink, that *I and Thou* flings me into
easy despair for green-gold gleans of acanthus, unfurled.

Is it true that to sing is also to touch.

Is it true that everything, always, everything is true.

You prepare to starve your body again.

You are violet or indigo intent.

That is, you are a missile or a murmur.

A spirit guide tells you *you're a tree* which you hear as *your body is wisdom undying.*

You know you're not dead, not yet lost fluorescence, not cave-dark.

Deep in your tree there's the spirit of a worried man grief-hinged because you will mis-tell his story, forget the blueberries summering the wood's ridge above a valley blackened with coal.

The tree can't be starved, already filled with a glint of ghosts dizzy with afterlife.

So, you starve alone, let your belly be a chamber.

You hollow your own blood in risk.

You purr sunlight in the reaches of who you become once you are empty.

That is, you purge the muggy August of Upper Appalachia.

The man's ghost watches you starve yourself.

He sees your body flush and hungry.

60

The shade opens for you.

You feel October in your throat.

The day is born.

The day she dies.

The damp orange molder of soybean fields.

Inhaled chill.

Your women make you cloaked, under-covered, an eclipse spread over light years, not lovely at all.

Silt is release, earth oozing effusive satin dirt.

Her armchair is a confluence of many rivers.

You smell her in your bedroom the weekend Kristen visits, thirty-three years after four aunts, three cousins and your mother sit in her apartment, the funeral done, palming knick-knacks, her smell settling also on their shoulders.

The annoyance of grief.

Not lovely at all, not swift.

In the law abiding background of the what-you-hadn't-imagined

a torch dims from tall licks of
tangerine rage to a small but balanced glow.

Your shore recedes from shawls of wave.

The tangle of your fertile future should funnel spine into being but
doesn't.

No one walks your halls.

The rupture cleaves to firmament, ovary-empty eyes.

You drive to the oldest tree in the forest, the first husband then a
white tail deer, the car-halting-moment, the bear, not a cub, not
grown, nimbus of what happens when we park, walk moss to the
hinterland-river's audible *ahh*, the minister -*hello*- then bound.

The bear is this past beginning.

That fern visions our *once again*.

Fill the minivan with every blouse.

Mortar the un-dimmed morning nameless.

Horizon, beacon-pink.

Far cattle.

The small planes.

64

He's shadow sown into your wandering thought.

You unravel the stitch.

You strike down the lash.

You un-gown your vows.

You pilfer the bleary moonlight, throat the burn he speaks.

You dig a sea.

You dig fathoms, stomach his perish, blurt his hail.

He's a tunnel toward release, a trapeze leaping—*leave*.

You gaggle your shame.

You dare his hunger.

You meander his peril with grief.

5.4 (a)

Regret is a bird beginning,

the wind that takes its nest, the fall that ends its life.

When the bird passes.

A slow and unfulfilled birth might be restless unbecoming.

A carcass means unconsummated living.

You discover the bird, a riddle of feathers, wilting bone flanking the gravel, a memory rehearsed restless as years.

In July, you refuse to go home, steal two books from the library, *The Photographs of Henri Cartier-Bresson* and Balzac's *Droll Stories*, neither of which you ever read, so full of peace and ruin.

Many years later, you buy replacements you never send, wilt guilt transmuted.

Precious death, this veil intending forgiveness.

Sun moves your shadow forward.

A dark ray outlined divine.

The bird is a message of regret.

The bird is a peace that detonates your timid doom, kindles eventual fire in the nest of your chest.

Peonies seem less conspiring, more bright.

A hawk feathers the morning.

Mist hovers visible.

Mountains sky plentitude.

Regret, a green apple, a runway of stone, a wink toward the vulture, festered coming loam—

5.4 (b)

A content warning for your session:

There was hope, but you were always late.

Her eyes, glass-wonder-sight.

You unfold like candor.

She nomenclatures you.

You tell her so.

Therapy is about finding whatever truths you've built into the walls of the home you've made of not dying.

Safety is a trigger, itself, illusive, backward, a trip from trauma to the moment before trauma, a volta that coils itself into helix-being, alive and mid-century, a building, a corner office, two walls of windows predicated on the axis she makes as two sides meet.

Outside, backdrop, rhododendron and spruce, hedge her.

You machine forward a verbal account of hop-along methods since
surviving, tell her you're building a house of prepositions:

I live again above the after.

 I live of things from the beyond before, during, over, me, throughout
—my windows, near, inhabit every room, are mirrors at night
following me to the door.

Q: Why do you need so many?
What one won't give me, another will, everything above and against
and again.

Q: Why do you need so many?
My windows inhabit every room.

 I'm throughout.

 I'm following, except my past.

 I'm beyond, except before, during, over.

You are always late (because therapy is whatever you built into the
walls of the home you've made of not dying).

 You machine-hop methods since surviving.

Safety-trigger, a retro-trek, trauma to the moment before, the volta.

Coil.

Helix.

Axis.

Where, two sides backdrop.

Where, rhododendron.

Spruce.

There can never be too many poems unless

there are too many poems with mourning
doves.

Their rising.

You wake, sun.

Suddenly, in the room, a day, again (though, the dove relents the joy
of ritual so each of its days dreads the next):

*Taxes: Monday / Strategies to Survive / Narcissistic Abuse / Writing
Prompt / Thank you to the Board for this Award / Drink Less—Buy
Less / go outside*

Years before, Janine drives her car into the side of a house the day after
her dormant bulb of post-adolescent grief spines its way along her inner
pathways, courses from heart chakra upward and down through each
root nerve, branching every limb of Janine until she's solely grief and
only-ness   for   the   rest   of   her   life.

Janine dies face down in November snow, not young, too young.

Grief is unkind in this way as a contagious regret of the sum.

I know her, but then, *She was.*

The refrain of her body slumbered and freezing in the yard.

You couldn't have stopped it.

The opposite of grief mutes an eventual return, a little bitter eclipse
made of so many weeks, of a slow something like—*a robin chooses to
perch on the deck-roof's gutter, a rust buff puffed against chill.*

Affliction recedes a bit to *after-robin,* then *chill.*

You're talking to a man who lives in the mountains,

somewhere past the gray misted foothills
beyond your window, snowcapped in April, the sound of his breath
carried despite warm-notes falling.

You are beautiful.

You wince under the weight.

A little lie ending in ripple, a flash.

Teeth that banister the cliff-edge of tongue, a reconciliation to rage.

He careens too close, imagines you too sweet.

Today, you search online for *the ugliest animals in the world.*

There's a tegu which looks like a dragon scaled black and lichen
green, not *handsome*—but handsome, the therapist you insist be black
and male, who says *cut yourself a break*—not *ugly,* nor is the hyena's
gnarl bent toward some carcass, nor the Marabou Stork's easter egg
head mottled violet against red, feminine, intimate as vultures.

Before she dies, your mother tells you no one ever called her beautiful
and you didn't say so then but should have because now—

The horseshoe bat is modest and vellum.

The warthog's arched mouth is rigid as a clavicle.

You are beautiful means you hate that man that lives on a mountain
who makes a narrative of *you.*

You are beautiful, naked mole rat, little star-nosed mole.

The most beautiful of the ugly have the smallest eyes.

A parasite is blind to ruin.

Open all of the drawers.

Wipe down the house.

Surviving *after* means finding him nowhere.

He touched so much.

You fail the day.

The glass he's left on the nightstand.

Sapphire streaks of light blessing blinds he rarely opened.

He only vacuumed in front of his favorite chair.

Ever.

The rug's rough.

The cushions keep his form.

Most things turn blue.

You cyan pleats of water under the shower's circular pulse.

The ceiling periwinkles last light.

The corners of the laundry room coddle midnight angles, shadow a moment you never share, teal on one wall, gray on the other.

The stairwell—*Get out.*

Each day, you want to forget the want of fig.

 You imagine you are also iris.

You want your filaments to give blue a run for its money, to out lapis lapis, to leverage the minutes of an Aquarius moon against your blooming sleep night after night after night, all timelines/universes, forever before.

 Your *after* is a siren in every room, the loft window's ice swollen at the sill.

 You shallow him each day, pinnacle *after* his turquoise, cull his indigo, *after* blue.

4.6

After a night of sleep-shopping,

                    you wake to two grocery bags on the porch, a
dozen individually packaged pieces of cake, a half-sheet of *Tres leches*,
four   scones.

Need   isn't   hearsay.

You   carry   them   to   the   trash.

Need isn't a tightrope of hunger strung between your sea and your
 moonlight.

It's a little shame unleashed in your throat.

It's a little empty.

It's an imprint of failed harvest.

Or peril, as in—*the dove won't look away.*

Somehow, you become a swarm webbed across a plane of singular
impulse—*eat (or perish) (or tunnel) (or plead).*

One summer you eat only carrots and Jell-O.

You   inward   your   want   until   you're   sated   with   loss.

You unmake yourself, pound after bleary pound, spine pressed against
the new world, stomach snailed against spine, edgewise and magic, not
fat   or   thin   or   fallow.

The first psychic says

your soul-mate's mind moves river-fast.

Another husband.

A streamflow and cycle.

When you divorce, you never miss his oblong impression in the dark.

You buffer disaster with bodies coming and going, metal-scent, almost-balmy-stink.

Your next psychic warns you of the moon but you stalk it anyway.

The next full moon is a Pink Moon and the last full moon is a Worm Moon.

The worst moon is in Libra and the best moon is in Leo (though no one agrees this is true).

You are older than you have ever been.

You've failed to find your lifetimes.

The lightning fields split and spark to hermitage even in the quick-safe archway of all past.

Your medium speaks lightly into the phone, traces your flesh with ancestors until you are a whole divination, a measure of their forward gathering silt-like tidal mouth of your body.

Be careful.

You will.

You will anchor yourself to ancient loss /or/ reason, align your regret with laughter, stop thinking of the moon until you're sure the moon thinks of you.

In the summer after, you knowingly hex every couple you see embrace,

you smite the air that keeps them, river their laughter into subway tunnels until they are reduced to screech and break.

You name them *loss* and *never,* incant their brindled end.

She   will   never   love   you.

The   beginning   is   always   a   lie.

A   bed   can't   muscle   the   night   into   your   halo.

When you read the words of a recluse poet, starkly casting, her boozy-lyric preening, you falter: *I hate sex, the man's mouth covering my mouth, the man's paralyzing body*—you can't peril her dismissal, can't fling her luck   into   the   street.

The trains balance the serendipity of your name against her future, plotted.

You allow each body to believe it's done something special, day-in, out, emancipate them to the sidewalk where the sun remains spellbound as they waver behind (virulent) lovey-dovey.

| They | never | find | the | ocean. |
| They | can't | ever | eat | enough. |

.

You pace from room to room

                         rearrange the articles of your most recent life.

Disown a vase.

Exile photos.

Sequester suits in the furthest closet.

Another husband.

Your ruins perch on the rim of anywhere you've made an everyday place.

She insisted on bathing you herself before sex and would sob after.

He loosened a brook within you until your breasts damned dark in the chasm where your heart had lived.

He was a shadow first and then a star.

When you say *moving* you really mean *shift*—void to velvet, wet to dark.

You weaponized magenta in the aquatic depths where all their bodies arrived, and lived, and died.

Cycle the recall, then, recalling, recall again.

Translate his red beard into a sonnet after.

You seized her open mouth and called it your own, grifted their only-ness with no guilt.

Say, *nothing of their eyes watched me loom.*

Say, *perhaps they forgot*—the umbrella, the blue dress, the taxonomy of twill, weft and want from which we free.

3.9

You feel the absence of a waterfall

                        as though a waterfall has at some point been part of
your life.

You feel a blaze kindle the ruin.

Animal flutes the bones of your body pitched as stinging.

You feel shackled.

You feel tackled.

You feel smacked, silver, pocked.

You whorl chasms and men.

You devour men.

You erase men.

You honor bodies of men.

You delete the bodies of men.

You phantom the bodies of men as a field wails its weeds.

As the weeds border your battle.

As you rattle a lark's flair.

As the lark razes the night.

As the night mimics her fight.

As her fight stipples the air.

You frail, wail.

You spark.

You slaughter morning's stark as though slaughter is part of your life.

You reel.

You raptor.

You jackknife your *she* who is wife.

3.2

You are never baneful.

You nail grief to the wall.

You wrap silence in lemon rind and linen then bury it in a moon's light.

You're a collective squall blood-buckled, a vision, a dream of a pebble —*good luck or bad luck*—

You wake craggy in the brain fog of near-birth, flounder in lace confines.

Puberty heathers the fields with ghosts of the soon-to-be dead.

Woe always makes its way.

The truck will hit us, you tell your mother and then she knows you know.

There is Lion's Mane where the bark slopes beneath a collar of moss.

A ceiling of red sky.

Another moon in Leo.

Hear me.

Fold the living earth into a congruent longing.

Reason with dark.

Plead as poets plead:

Hear us.

Hear us among the fleshy hierarchies.

88

Catch a glimpse of water swirling.

The porcelain toilet lost against light.

You peel your nightgown off, flush it away.

Your body supine, landscaped in your father's arms, muddled, a quake
sleepwalking through a year on earth.

You undress and piss in the same dream.

You don't know how sleep rehearses your future.

You look for a dog you never had, give up sugar, not sure how to word
anything but the tricky end.

Your bedroom looms over the bed.

You sleep alone even before he's gone as though you'd never found a
man reading Albert Camus on the steps leading to your room:

The Stranger

Copper corduroys.

Pocket fray, shaped like a book.

You learn in a language of dragons he is *un homme du midi*, a fulcrum that kindles olfactory recall whenever you sip coffee, ask *are you hungry?*

He smelled like butter.

He held you like your father did, carefully, as though you were a sharp thing needing to be dulled.

Murmur your way back.

                          Everything that begins with desire will fail
and still you know less each year.

You think about rereading *The Education of Henry Adams* again,
remember something about Henry learning to ride a bicycle as an
adult, the skittish posture of his wobbling brink, a shadow against
horizon.

He knew less each year.

The obscene persistence of privilege reduced to a blink.

You subscribe to *The Atlantic* again though mostly read just article
titles.

How to Want Less mentions St Thomas Aquinas, The Rolling Stones,
Buddha, and Jean-Paul Sartre in the first 100 words.

How impossible, *less,* so un-male, except for Buddha who genders
violet at best, who hangs at the outer reaches of *what.*

Buddha-soul.

Buddha-glitch waiting.

Sir and *Mister* and *Yes,* the pay-wall of patriarchy you only unlock with a body.

You imagine the grind as pleasure like a rock-dove saying *who-who, who, who.*

Disruption scallops your near-future-igneous remains, not so much *knowing* as *forgetting to forget* to never not be angry again.

_____

2.9

Forward

You won't remember this day.

The   snow   drifts   fine   and   horizontal.

The   wind   has   no   purpose   but   to   recall   arctic   chill.

You   expect   magic   to   honeycomb   morning   because   you've   always   expected   too   much.

Your   husband   won't   leave.

The sheer will of a far city calls you home, the ruined valley, the
shanked   streets,   the   heaven   mixed   into   mortar.

But,   the   woods.

The   trail   ravaged   in   thorn.

The   cursive   ferns   ruffled   to   near-dark.

Cave   your   rattle.

Sheer   your   breath.

The desert solitudes perpetually—

Your rib cage is empty so you bring two bagel sandwiches to the homeless woman sitting in front of Ozzie's Pub.

She   runs   away.

You chase her down determined to fill your chest with giving.

The   street   blinks.

You, waving white take-out bags in the air, stunted as she refuses your kind   fiction,   shelters   herself   against   your   wound.

But,   the   city.

The   freeway   can't   remember   your   pace.

The condominium sill has forgotten the orchids, phalaenopsis, moth flowers.

Your   husband   insists   and   then   lets   them   die.

The moment of *no* throbs, there and here, pulses bone-ruins for fear of dying   which   is   conventional   and   unsophisticated.

But,   the   woods.

A   piney   mosaic   finds   its   way   toward   gutters.

You sleep in leaves, imprints, the subway's deciduous fringe, chestnut
h   u   s   k   .

An un-homed woman eats a sandwich and you're stupidly relieved, as
though she'd been waiting for you, as though you are her absent sky.

The   irrigation   spillway   conjoins   wheat   fields.

You remember this day but only his heart's halo:

It's   brassy   like   a   bullet   once   he's   gone.

2.22.22

Acknowledgements

p. 23 lines quoted from Louise Glück's "Mock Orange," from *The First Four Books of Poems* (Ecco Press, 1995)

p. 34 lines quoted from Kazim Ali, from *Silver Road: Essays, Maps, and Calligraphies* (Tupelo Press, 2018)

p. 36 in reference to Donna Shymanski, my best friend that summer.

p. 39 in reference to and in honor of my colleague, Noah Eli Gordon.

p. 50 in reference to Kristin Peterson Kaszubowski.

p. 89 in reference to Henry Adams' *The Education of Henry Adams*, original publication in 1907.

Ruth Ellen Kocher is the author of eight books, *godhouse* (Omnidawn, 2023), *Third Voice* (Tupelo Press, 2016) winner of the PEN Open Book Award, *Ending in Planes* (Noemi Press, 2014), *Goodbye Lyric: The Gigans and Lovely Gun* (Sheep Meadow Press, 2014), *domina Un/blued* (Tupelo Press, 2013), Dorset Prize winner and the 2014 PEN/Open Book Award, *One Girl Babylon* (New Issues Press, 2003) Green Rose Prize winner, *When the Moon Knows You're Wandering* (New Issues Press, 2002), and *Desdemona's Fire* (Lotus Press 1999).

She has been awarded fellowships from the National Endowment for the Arts, the Cave Canem Foundation, MacDowell, and Yaddo and is a Contributing Editor at Poets & Writers Magazine. She has been named a Distinguished Professor of English at the University of Colorado where she teaches Poetry, Poetics, and Literature.

Archon / After
by Ruth Ellen Kocher
Cover art: Ruth Ellen Kocher
Cover design by Ruth Ellen Kocher and Laura Joakimson
Cover typeface: Courier
Interior design by Laura Joakimson
Interior typeface: Dapifer and Courier

Printed in the United States
by Books International,
Dulles, Virginia on Acid Free Archival Quality Recycled Paper

Publication of this book was made possible in part by gifts from
Katherine & John Gravendyk in honor of Hillary Gravendyk,
Francesca Bell, Mary Mackey, and The New Place Fund

Omnidawn Publishing Oakland, California
Staff and Volunteers, Fall 2024
Rusty Morrison & Laura Joakimson, co-publishers
Rob Hendricks, poetry & fiction editor,
& post-pub marketing
Jeffrey Kingman, copy editor
Sharon Zetter, poetry editor & book designer
Anthony Cody, poetry editor
Liza Flum, poetry editor
Kimberly Reyes, poetry editor
Elizabeth Aeschliman, fiction & poetry editor
Sophia Carr, production editor
Jennifer Metsker, marketing assistant
Rayna Carey, marketing assistant
Katie Tomzynski, marketing assistant